LOVERS
AND
CELEBRATIONS

JOEL RUDINGER

DEARBORN PRESS
CHICAGO

I wish to thank the Ohio Arts Council for an Individual Artist's Grant that provided time to work on some of these poems and to the Virginia Center for the Creative Arts where several of these poems were conceived. I also wish to thank Bowling Green State University for a faculty development grant which made my presence at the Virginia Center for the Creative Arts possible. And a special thanks to Dennis Horan for his help in the darkroom.

Some of these poems have appeared in the *Colorado North Review, Cornfield Review, New York Quarterly, Firelands Review, Poetry Project Two, The Lamp, Kudzu, Inkstone, Capricorn, Poems 1978-1983* edited by Bob Fox, and Margaret Christy's *Quest for Centenarians.*

Dearborn Press
127 N. Dearborn, Suite 222
Chicago, IL 60602

ISBN 0-918342-20-1

This book is for my daughters Jennifer and BethAnne
and for all the other life-lovers who helped me into and
through the last decade.

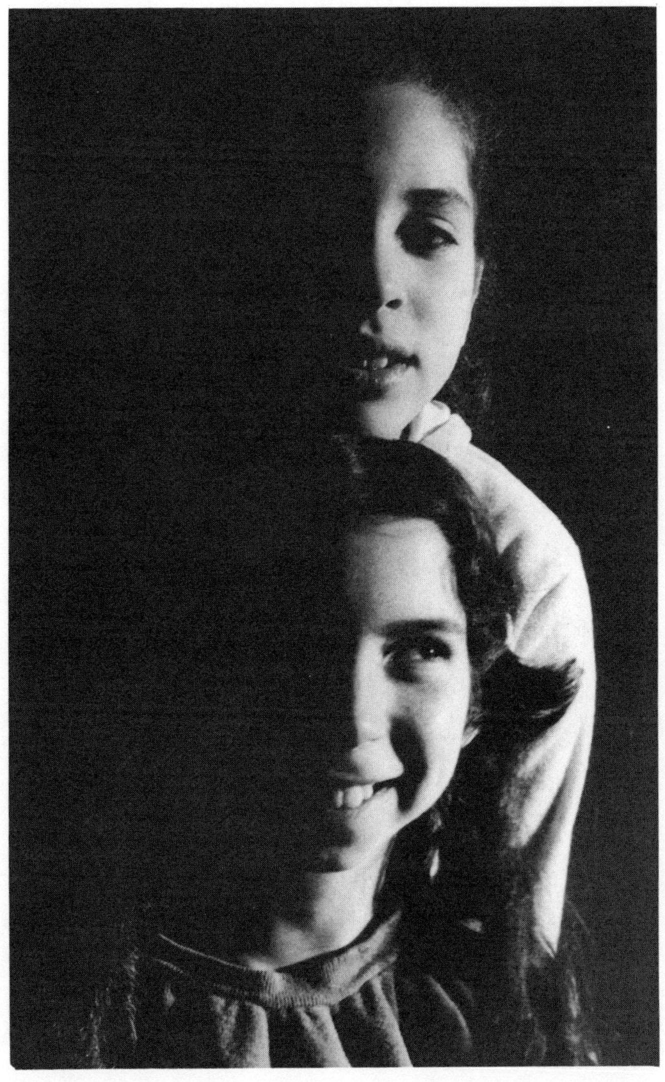

"Happy are those who dream dreams and are ready to pay the price to make them come true."

— L. J. Cardinal Syenens

CONTENTS

LOVERS
AND
CELEBRATIONS

I

THE GREAT POSITIVE

BLUE LOVERS

"no pat philosophies apply"

(for Krys)

"I have been with you before," she said.
"We were together in a different life.
Once you were my King of Hearts,
a man who took me out of my shackles
and let me rise up out of my fears."

It was the end of sunset.
I felt the red mist falling through the lake.
The sun sank slowly in the distant haze
and I did not believe in her continuity of time
or that my being was continous.
I did not believe that I had lived before, breathed, loved
somewhere out of this world, beyond my memory.
"I would surely know," I said, "and deeply feel it."

She turned and spun me in the vortex of her eyes.
"This I know and have for centuries known
and you will come to know it.
If not now, then soon."

How easy to forget her words, I thought.
But her iridescent eyes grew deep and black
and when I lay me down to sleep,
back, back into a midnight darkness,
I saw myself in a raging river
where silver marlins sang with children's voices,
millenial fish that leaped above me
their contrails slashing the sky with rainbow.

"Our worlds unfold and overlap the lives of all our
    deaths,"

she said. "We pass away a thousand times to live again.
We grow in our return."

A ghost soul-process or a man—I wondered if it
    mattered what I was.
Because here she was with me beneath a river of stars
and I saw us only in the water of the sky,
two warm bodies colored by the hues of light,
orange, red, violet, and then
sea birds touching in circular motion,
blue lovers waiting for the coming of night.

BLESS RELAXES

Swimming naked at the bottom of a wide blue pool
my students and I swim together.
We move like a school of shiners,
turning as one, turning again as one.
Our eyes are in love with all of each other
in our open body hello non-touch
but palpable kisses.
Our minds are the water we swim in
together like a school of shining
brilliant dolphins. Hours pass.
Not a ripple breaks the surface of the water.
There is so much beauty here,
so much harmony of movement,
there is so much water.

LOVERS

We can be lovers even entering from separate doors,
be of any color, any size, ageless,
lovers of deeply different bodies.

Tall and dark with tall and dark,
tall and dark with short and light,
we need not speak the same language, or speak at all.
We can be mute, we can be blind,
in silent darkness we can know each other's gold and
   silver tones.

My flesh can take your song and give it back again,
turn the rushing impulse round
with a stroke of hair, a kiss,
a long slow upward brush of fingers.

We can join together in this private time
and bring our secrets to each other's arms.
The floor is moss, the air is pine and mountain
and the wide earth spreads waiting.

COMING FOR DINNER

This time let's take our time with cooking.
We'll let night surround us like an oven
and we'll rise together, like yeast,
and long lay to heaven.
Then when we're up, we'll set the table
with homemade bread, some cheese, your lemon cake.
I'll serve the pasta, you pour red wine,
and we'll sit next to each other in sable
robes and candlelight.
                              I'll give. You take.
A body is a wonderful thing. Take mine.

POETRY

This line is the shadow of her mouth,
the rhythm of her lips, soft and narrow
holding round the warm impression of my love.
I kiss her lips glistening with gentle yes.
She kisses me back with myself.

Her white hands are stanzas,
fingers softly spread
cupping me around my waist.
Her arms, flowering vines, hold me up.
I do not fall with her. She keeps me safe.

She is the cream of moonlight
spread on the Pacific.
The sand of her hair is all my beach.
My belly is her canoe.
We become each other's theme.
In the deep iambics of the waves she rides me out
and we paddle and coast over crest upon crest.
The surging sea climbs the rocks at shore beyond us
and washes itself in its own salt.

Her legs are as long as mine.
Our mutual thighs make us equal where they join.
Her poem is in me; I am
also in her poem. We are
refrains beyond myth, past symbol.

We are arms, legs, bellies, smothering hair.
And hands. Hands subtler than sight.
They are kisses intangible, swifter than couplets.

And after, there is more than just stiff traces of the
    night,
no hard lines of rigid form.
Our sheets are flowing poems, lyrical. And all
the run-ons are the touches of our tongues.

NO POEM

Dawn in an empty room.
Bare walls.
A basket of dirty laundry.

I don't love you, she said.
I don't love you, I said. We never said we did.
It won't work, she said.
There never was anything to work, I said. Don't worry
    about it.

She put her glass down on the carpet and leaned back
    into the cushions.
Her long hair fell like a curtain over her face.

I should go now, I said.
The wine was warm and sour.
It has nothing to do with you, she said.
Her eyes were open under her fallen hair.
She was trying to look out the window, toward the
    sky coloring up slowly beyond the east.

I'm just afraid.

Something was outside in her dark.
She was very quiet.
All right, I said. Let's call the poem finished.
Yes, she whispered. You make it easy. Thank you.
A tiny sun broke through the trees. Something safe.
Kiss me, she said.

SKETCH ONE

We lay in the day-lit room under a thin quilt.
The quiet face beside me moved.
Her eyes opened to the ceiling.
A smile came and went. I felt her mouth.

It seems that all my friends are my lovers, she said.

Outside her window a car drove through rain.
All your friends are lovers?
What I mean is, I don't have many friends.
I'm your friend, I said.
And you're my lover.

Dim light behind the drawn shade. Turned down gold
   light everywhere.

It's odd, she said, that we never made love before.
I thought about that for a long time.
Not so odd, I said. Not really so odd.

She closed her eyes (yes) and in so doing
opened us to everything that followed.

SCENES AND INNUENDOS ON A SUMMER NIGHT

At the far edge of the river
even at midnight, outside
the Twine House, the Huron lime plant
fumes its sulphur starward.
A diesel dozer grinds down loudly spotlighted
against the hard tits of gravel mountains.
In the vast foreground, stern props churning,
The *Robert L. Thompson* maneuvers
a slow long turn in the black channel.

Inside the Twine House lounge, soft and sexy
I lay hands on this one's hips
as they pass in the sweet jazz
rock hot disco light.
This wife, this slim Scheherezade
turns into voluminous chords.
Hips or lips, I lay hands on.
Her deep brown eyes dance and conjure
a thousand and one strategies.

Good night, ladies. Good night, friends.
The *Robert L. Thompson* has made it into port.

II

Whatever you do, feel!
This is our only life.

"WALK"

for Susan H.

Where does a man go when he finally leaves?
If he is wise, he faces East and kneels to himself.
God sits in a mirror and is himself.
Only when a man pulls free can he find
the Truth is what he's always thought
but couldn't know, what he's always known
but couldn't think.
This is the riddle of the act of leaving:
life blows apart and comes together again
in time, whole and new and tight.

Experience had me convinced that Truth was sad
and that I'd wither with sadness
until I turned myself off with a .38.
That I had come to believe
until you came to me, Susan.
Like the feared angel whose time had come
you led me to the ocean on a stormy day
and showed me how to think of freedom.

The freezing air, the waves of the hurricane
boiling over Virginia Beach,
and the close hotel room that smelled
like the sex den of a succubus
converged and lifted me high enough to see
what had been a shrouded tower
too far out in mist to understand.

Hand in hand we went looking for dinner
and I talked routines, obligation, duty, sadness.
Later, head by head we lay together
and when you said so simply in the night

that one word I had never heard, never listened to,
I knew that you were right.
I had only to see it done and it was done.
And then after I left and returned to Ohio
I said what it was that you'd let me see
and it was done. I was free.
Then I had only to say Goodbye.

And where does a man go when he finally leaves?
If he is wise, he faces West and smiles to himself
and sees the world lying like a carpet of soft grass
waiting for his own precious godly unencumbered step.

RESURRECTION TIME

How long have my daughters slept?
Has it been a year since I kissed them good morning?
Their voices whimper from leaden covers,
from separate rooms at the top of the black tower.
They have been fighting to wake up, but their struggles
have driven them deeper into night.
Oh my children, wake up. Wake up.

I'd rip the mufflers off their beds
if I could reach them, shake them firmly
by their bones and say love, startle them up
and squeeze them to my heart again. To my heart.

I think about them every day,
count days and ignore the days I count.
And still the calendar thickens with my blood
and grows slowly heavy like a nasty sponge
trapped, like Sisyphus, on the wrong side of Lethe.
Has it been a year since I kissed them good night?

Yes, a year, and it is surely time
to bring them back to sunlight,
give them a honey breakfast, touch their petals open,
trace the lines of peace again down their cheeks.
Tomorrow, tomorrow I will grow legs back
and attack the tower's slippery dark.
Tomorrow I will bring them back to life.
Tomorrow, I will take them back.

THE POET WANDERS ALONG THE SHORE

Her legs no longer flash in the dark lake.
Joel now knows how much came from the moon.
A new wind hardens to stone like a mouth.
The woman of this man's dreams is dust.

There is a new emptiness about the sky.
He has no fear of losing the unreal.
Bad rhythm is awful in a dancer's kiss.
White bones have long jumped in an empty house.

Why are the dark children surrounded by angry birds?

The tides arrive and leave again like strangers.
Sand at the edge of the world gets wet and dries
while echoes whisper from space that Time supplies.
Clearly now he sees natural elements unite
to separate: land from water, the moon from night.

SKETCH 2

We were walking through the dust, through the valley of
   the Dead.
I mean, she said, you have to be assertive. There is
   nothing I won't do when I'm away.
What? I said. Away from what?
Behind us was the Pyramid of the Sun. Dark children
   surrounded us selling bright angry birds, drawings
   by their fathers, silver bracelets, baked red muted
   figurines of Mayan gods, polished obsidian faces,
   identical small bodies wrapped in rubbing cloths—
   the black hands of the children rubbing rubbing.
I mean, she said, I get what I want.
Over us a hollow sun, a hot blue sky.
We had been there hours. She looked at me.
You are red. You are burning, she said.
Yes, I said. I am burning. We are both burning.
I'd better wear my coat tonight, she said. It will be cold.
   Moonlight is cold on burnt skin.
The hands of the children hidden in their cloths,
   rubbing rubbing,
and the sun hot above.

FLAMES

Sometimes work is not enough.
Work does not quell urgency.
Instead, words suffocate.
Out of multitudinous high-pitched sonographs and
    dictaphones
endless metallic consonants
issue from mechanical lips.
Then, the walls of the office threaten
like cymbals poised to shock
every idea and feeling and moment back
into the black heat of inner space.
Every room, day or night, day and night, is prison.
Outside, only, in open air
is the illusion of freedom.

This is the battle of a man with himself,
his fortieth fear of a shrinking life.
This is the blameless, innocent blunted rage of the bull
    caught in the underbrush,
of the shadowy swallow that weaves and dashes
    in the violent sky before nightfall.
This is the sensual lust that engulfs the moth in flames
    for its passion of light.

A man, also, is drawn to flames,
bright openings in the walls of night,
in search of any girl's voice, any woman's eye,
whether it sees him or not, or will ever see him.
Like the shallow red siren of the cat trapped
    pacing, shut behind locked doors,
a man's battle is one with the animal's rage
carved out of silence.

Tonight there is a woman with long dark hair
reading, framed in a bright window.
It is almost enough to watch her,
but soon the light will flicker and go out,
darkness will return and surround him like a throat.
It will be all he can do not to be its shout.

MORNINGS WITH SUZZANNE

Suzzanne is sleek with pride
and runs in burnished silk,
yet sweeps the kitchen floor for me
between slow sips of milk.
But I do not love her.
I'd rather love a stone than her.

I've watched her slink about
late edges dimly lit,
aware that I'm aware so that
she prisoners my night.
I'd rather love a stone than her.
She stares at me, at nothing.

Then, then she comes home mornings—
those little teeth of ice—
and spreads upon my tablecloth
ten daggers stained with mice.
She stares at me, at nothing
with a stare that gristles bone.

She stares at me, then nothing,
and penetrates for hours
a statue caught within a glass;
my eyes draw out to hers.
I do not love her.
She loves herself alone.

THE PERFECT MARRIAGE

i love you, he said,
and with a rose in his teeth he died.

MOVING OUT

Moving out in circles
wolves around prey
husbands and wives
women and men
daughters and fathers
fox and chickens
the forest surrounds the lake
the clouds around the earth
the earth and the sun
the night cups out the day
and leaks it back again

Goodbye is what he says
this Tuesday
in the morning
on the way to the foothills of the city
packing up
taking all the bags and books
all the loose change
stuffs his satchel with pockets
If he comes back
goodbye is what he'll say
again

Moving out or moving away
coming back in the flesh
staying away in the mind

barriers

Love is a method of survival
a technique like climbing a rope
hand over hand
foot on foot

into the light

The physical world
comes but once in a life.

III

The sun comes up in many ways.

THE BED

The man who died here was like me.
He curled under his blanket on long nights
and lay alone when the moon was full
sometimes. On hot nights in the small room
he spread his fingers on the wall, breathed in
under the shifting gables of this old house,
sweating deeply into the mattress.

When I arrived to take the room,
the bed sighed to me like a dreaming stranger.
They say he weighed two hundred pounds
and kept alone to starve the fat off,
that he lost an extra body and its soul,
that he sweated away half of the man
he was, that he died alone in the bed,
a quiet contemplative bone.

When I stretched out in the bed
the first night, my body hit the floor.
All the support slats were broken.
No matter how I lay, I gathered
in the middle of his grave and slept
a deep and strangely peaceful sleep.
I recall that I came in middle March
and the first morning sun blazed through
the bedroom window with such a light
that the lime green walls and ceiling
took in that light and glowed like a Sunday springtime
    forest.
The warmth that rose like a spirit from the bed
took me up out of whomever I was
and when I arose, I rolled up ready
out of the sagging mattress, bright
to the rim of a new day.

GENESIS

Who is this entering man in the white smock?
He lifts the lid of the clay bin
and gouges out chunks of damp mud.
He heaps clay back and stirs the bin with a trowel.
The room is silent except for the suck of earth
being ripped from its soft moisture.
He has not yet turned on the light.
It is not yet time.

Armatures rise like crosses on their pedestals
empty of idea, of touch, of form.
They rise in shadow, skeletons of potential
in the hollow room.

He, too, hears the voices coming.
The first one in flicks on the light
and the studio fills with speech.
All the young artists baffle their tongues,
babble their languages.
There is too much talk; nothing can yet be heard.

The man in white turns and raises his trowel.
A sudden quiet. Expectation.
A signal is coming.
Everyone is excited. Everyone waits, anticipates.
It comes. It comes.
He has chosen this moment to nod Yes.

Today they are working in clarity.
The hands of the angels have entered the bin.

I WAS THINKING OF APPLES

I was thinking of apples,
red apples, red with yellow
and yellow touched with green
specks and specks of gold,
soft gold, the kiss of birds
to hint where sweetness lies.

Apples cut and sugared,
browned and moistened in a pie,
cinnamon and crust, warm
steam rising like a tongue
licking the air, devouring it.
Soft apples, sliced hot,
baked, gold with juice of lemon.

Lemon in a pie with apples.
Such a way to think of apples.

TIME IS ALL I NEED
AND THEN THE WORLD WILL COME

Time is all I need and then the world will come.
Time, time, the world is made of time
and the time will come when all the world is time,
and Time will come and come in time.

The waters of the ocean wash at time
and clean it silver and green with motion.
The motion is of time and washes the world
which comes in green, in silver.
Time is the world turned silver.

Silver silence, silent time, time is washing
the world of the earth. Time is the water.
Water is all I need and then the earth will shine.
Water, water, the earth is made of water
and the water will come when it is time.
Water will come when time turns prayer.
The earth will come and come in water.

Water is the truth that washes the earth silver.
The clean earth is green and silver to the truth.
Silence is the truth. Truth is always silent
and its motion is like water,
the water which comes in time.

Truth is all I need and then the world will come.
Truth, truth, the water is made of earth
and the time will come when all the earth is water,
and the truth will come and come in silver time
in a body of motion, in a wash of silence.

Time is all I need and then the truth will shine.
Time and truth, the world is made of earth
and the truth will come when all the world is water.
The silver will come and come in time and truth.

Truth is silver water washing earth in Time.
Silence is the earth in silver water prayer.
In silver water, the earth will emerge shining
and the wash of truth in silent time
will be the world of truth and all I need of truth,
water all I need of prayer,
and prayer, silver water, all I need of time.

SOLO I WILL STAND IN THE WINDS
THAT CHOOSE TO TAKE ME

Solo I will stand in the winds that choose to take me.
Stand me in the winds. Will I solo in the winds that take.
Stand in the winds, solo I will choose to solo.
Solo in the winds that choose to take me I will stand.

Stand. I will solo in the solo winds to choose.
Take me, solo; solo will I stand in the winds that choose;
choose to take me, winds, that solo I will stand.
I will stand in the winds that solo choose to take me.

Take me, solo, choose. Solo will the winds to choose.
Take me, I will stand in the solo winds that choose to
    solo.
Winds to take and solo will I take to stand.
Winds, winds, in solo stand I take to me that choose to
    will.

Solo in the will, choose to stand the winds that take.
Solo I will solo in the winds to solo in the solo winds.
Winds, winds' will, I stand to take me solo.
Take me, take me, stand I wind, choose me solo,
    solo winds.

I will choose the winds' solo, solo choose the will.
Choose to take me, in the winds that will me solo.
That stand I take, the solo winds that choose to will me,
To choose me, to stand in the will, stand in the solo will.

HUSH, THE GIRLS ARE SLEEPING

They are above me.
The peace of their dreams passes upwards
and somewhere there is a key,
a magic touch that first set their bodies in motion,
that put there the living breath
and started their soft miracles bellowing
through days and nights
as clocks tick continuous in perfect balance
as though each void in sound and physical nature were
    calculable
and filled exactly by its perfect positive and opposite
    shape.

Then in the night I hear it and sit up,
the semi's thunder,
the ponderous echo of steel and engine.
Tires whine under the heavy friction—
hot, dry, smokeless, powered full throttle.

A chant comes to me: the child, the child, the child,
the child at night.
                    A faint cry, electric,
a faint scream over the far concrete
across the field
tremelos, under the stars, into the distance.

It is gone now. And the flatlands of the desert
illuminate silence. I hear what I should not hear.
In day, silence shimmers up in rainbows of heat
but at night the sands are cold
and flesh shocks up the sluggish rattler,
which crawls anywhere towards the nearest warmth.
And I am it.

Still their beauty sleeps above me
and the whispers of their dreams
are like angels rising out of chaos.
I want to write about my daughters as they sleep.
I want to hold in the space of this page forever
the blessings of their breath and the power their souls
    make
escaping constantly from their fragile lungs.

The peace of their dreams evolve
like slow electric kisses passing down a length of cool
    wire,
unwinding from within the narrow arches of their secret
    minds.

But again the earth intrudes. There is not their lulling
but the clash,
not the touching silence
but the omnipotent death of the red desert
and the unholy slithering guiltless lust of the serpent.
And it is this that I am forced to know:
that I am the soul of the body that calls the serpent
    forth;
that I am the generation of my body's fire;
that I am the fire itself,
the hell from which the fire comes;
desolation, blight, the incarnation of the terrible heat,
death in the sand, the beast, myself the snake, the
    earth.

And yet
they sleep above me still,
innocence gently pressed beneath fleet eyelids,
their quiet fluted wings of tiny evenings,
early spring. It is the touch of the thing

that whispers down to me, saving,
with the voices of angels.

DARK LADY

(for t.l.)

When the horizon meets beyond the light
the dark lady rises from the candle's glow
and leaves the table rustling her wide skirts.
One pale hand brushes over her black hair
and her blue canary trickles from its cage.
There is in her the beginning of a song, but
"Sunset is sunrise in another world," she says,
"and the stars are nothing new but disappear."
Moon at crack of dusk. A summer owl. She turns.
I rise until my candles flicker and go out.
The fires in her tiara blaze like stars.

I SAILED BEYOND THE SEA OF DARKNESS

I sailed beyond the sea of darkness
and Death was a beacon
rising like a white shaft
out of my mind's eye.

There was no reason to mourn you
alive and breathing on the other end.
The plumbline of my world
cast a golden shade.

Such a twinkle had gone up.
Smoke was all there was
and then the wind came clean
to split the air glistening.

I sailed without a boat.
Shifts of memory flowed out,
took me where I had to go,
where I am going now.

No breath.
No blood.
I wait with a calm eye, a cool rush
of something, something love.

The sea of darkness is a fear
only in the mind. Turn it around
to find the thing we yearn for:
Joy.

IV

We will never chart the dark side of the sun.

SITTING FOR MARGARET

"No, no," she says. "Don't move. It's hard
enough to draw someone under sixty."
So I sit, quietly aware that shadows creep toward me
as her pencil whispers over the rough paper.

"How do you see me?" I ask without words.
The pencil growls and scratches deep into the fiber.
"You never know," she says, "how it will turn out."

"Old men are easiest to draw." She glances up.
All their years of work and loss, pain and loving
trench their faces with lines of a lost beauty.
It stands out like rows of wheat unharvested
withered from too much richness.
And, Joel, I have looked often into old men's eyes;
those deep wrinkles drawn down by gravity and time
frame not eyes, no eyes, but an immortal soul."

Suddenly her fingers jam; the pencil's lead snaps off.
"No, no," she says. "The lip. The eyes. And—here,
    look—
something else about the mouth."
"No smile," I say. "That's not what I meant at all."
"It's so hard to do someone under sixty," she says
    again.
"Experience has not yet undone the sinews. Your face
has not yet unfolded to your grace."

It's five o'clock. She packs away her pencils, gum and
    pad.
"We'll try again tomorrow." Then she goes.
Gone, I wonder blankly where the smile was I thought I
    had.
And she knows.

THE INSPECTION

There is a pebble on my shoe.
I am, in fact, being stepped on.
I have stood here only a second
but certainly, without doubt,
this pebble has gathered itself
and has fastened down on me.

But now observe how with my thumb and pointer,
softer than a child plucks a puffer from her sleeve,
I lift this pebble gently, gently
raise it to my nose and balance it
there.

First one eye stares, then the other.
Never both at once.
Two eyes cannot see it balancing
on the end of my nose; two eyes
focus quite beyond it, missing completely
what this pebble is.

What *is* this pebble? Indeed, what is
any pebble? The answer eludes me.
My left eye closes, my right eye squints.
Up the pebble jumps. Absurd.

And now with sudden little wings
it hovers and is gone.

DISCHARGE FROM THE ASYLUM

My room is small and green. And it is mine.
I can go to hide in it and hide alone.
But now the hole is locked and Mona keeps the key.
I love her little pocket. I love her secretly.

The nurses stand erect. They line the hall.
Their big utensils hid behind them scar the wall.
They do not look. They do not see. Not see.
Who passes close before them? It is me.
My eyes, too, I keep them straight ahead
to pass by these white people whose eyes are dead.

Then down the distant hall I see the door.
I feel my knee joints freeze and lock. I feel the floor.
My fingers on the tile are smooth and cold.
My face upon the polished floor is old.

Shadows catch my fingers. The door glass is ajar.
I count a hundred shoelaces. The door is far.

O O WONDER WOMAN

I love the savage eagle spread golden over your breasts,
the hard blue shining of your eyes, your calm mouth,
milk white Amazon thighs bound tight in sleek acrylon
    ready for action.
And the way you wave your shimmering bracelets,
bright against the Nazi bastards trying to gun you down,
their puny bullets flashing off your wrists like diamonds.
And your legs, those legs, those exquisite pitons of
    Amazon power
all-woman long, hiding the secret amulet
where the great star hangs in conjunction with Venus,
a deep and wild promise.
I love also your golden lasso.
Take it, o take it, and put it on
me; bind me and squeeze out my truth,
but let your questions be kept low, Wonderous,
and non-political. Let them be about us
or about the length of your red leather boots
or the whips of your ebony hair
or the talons of the mighty eagle as he hovers above
    the mountains.

RED WATER MITE

Against imaginary currents—
movement on neither surface
nor subsurface, nor a wind to pile
up ripples, nor fishtails to thrash out
underwaves—this small shocked thing, this al-
most invisible red mite persists.

A pin feather in the surface dust
of the pond still from dawn, still
is still at dusk, but in its shadow's
changing angle the furious red
speck swims, swims, swims in endless struggle,
its legs like oars on a foundering ship.

Three legs and three legs, three legs and three
legs paw, flash in their dark sea.
This vermilion is more set in its
nothing jaw than a salmon beating
its body blood raw making painful
headway upstream, in touch with the fear.

Not bravery, not truth, but Must keeps
it, like an electric toy,
short-circuited, burning, glow-jammed in
perpetual motion. The hugeness
of its need, the instinct of its hope
is fire to the mountain of its lust.

Tomorrow I know it will be gone.
This bug less than bug, its halves
like hearts, cannot survive its frantic
pace, which must wear it surely down to
death, though it sends me unsatisfied
home in darkness, and outlasts the sun.

DENALI

How many years have I remembered the mountain?
Denali the natives call it, the magnificent rock.
Standing in its shadow made me feel like a ram
aching to leap its steepest slopes or gamble
my life to soar like an eagle over its desert
of ice chasms and cravasses. Who could publish

such a feeling of wild nature untamed? To publish
a climber's memoirs could never do justice to that
    mountain.
There is the secret of Time buried deep in its rock
and no man can know the secret like the white ram
which haunts its cloud-banked slopes. The rams gambol
in the bright sun of morning from the heights of the
    desert

and, like the sun, shine down. They are no desert
animals, but pure spirit, pure nature. If I publish
any poem about Denali, the ram will be part of the
    mountain
for he is the soul that quickens the rock into more than
    rock.
Once on the North Slope I came face to face with a
    white ram,
an ancient three-curl ram who never had to gamble

his honor with a man on his homeland. Nor was there a
    gamble
with me, for I stood in awe in the vast desert
of his white landscape, wordless. Nor would he publish
his mute secret of winter, the real meaning of the
    mountain.
I stood rock still and my shadow was the image of a rock
caught in motion between two motions. I became that
    ram

though in imagination only. Denali's secrets, the soul
    of the ram,
remained beyond. And I could neither freeze nor gamble
on the wind and move toward him, towards his icy desert
into the mouth of the cloud. My own eyes I knew would
    publish
what I wanted. I raised my hand to shield the mountain,
then in the dizzying height I started to rock.

Cold air, ice, breathless, in the snow I hit a rock
as I fell, and the spirit that came before me was a ram
whose eyes were blue. May I never again gamble
on sunrise if he didn't come to me, sprawled on his
    desert,
an alien man-intruder, hungry to publish
this ram, this secret of Denali, this awesome mountain.

I will never forget that mountain or the gamble
I took clinging to that rock, the only handlock on that
    desert
of vertical ice, nor the god-white ram who gave me final
    leave to publish.

THE CITY BROTHER
AND THE COUNTRY BROTHER

How can you stand it? he said.
It grows on you, I said.
There are no buildings here, he said.
In Huron we watch the sun rise, I said.
But the people, he said. The people. Where are the
    people?
They, I said, are all in their houses making love.

There's no traffic, he said. It's so quiet.
Look there, I said. See those two cars by the light?
See them?
No, over there, ahead.
I see them, he said.
Check your watch, I said.
It's five o'clock.
Yes, I thought so, I said. That was rush hour.

Jack Addams had just turned eighty-three. He and his
wife Dora were shuffling towards us in their blue warm-
up suits, slowly, single file over the two lane bridge.
When we passed them in the car, they had stopped to
look over the railing at the water in the creek, at the ice
jams collected along the edge in the brown reeds sur-
vived from summer.

Look, he said. People.
Those are joggers, I said.
He looked around at them as we went by.
They'd be dead in Chicago, he said. They're not
    moving.
They're jogging nevertheless, I said. Things slow down
    here.

We saw a dog.
You never see a dog in Chicago, he said.
I love dogs, I said. Big ones hang around the lake. We
    all love them.
Where is the lake? he asked.
Off to the right, I said, between the houses.

Down angled stone streets, small houses close together,
trees bare in winter scattered in natural disorder,
ice-covered this day the long miles of solid water
usually the hue of emeralds in clouds, but bluer often,
    often greener.

No downtown, traffic, people, noises, he said. How can
    you stand it? I'd go crazy.
It grows on you, I said.

WHAT THE SPOOKS SAID

Don't go into the cemetery at night, they said.
There's something there that takes your breath away.
Or if you do, take care to be silent.
Don't open your mouth to breathe
for the black flies attack at dark
and go for holes in the open face,
and if none is showing they will bore them deeply there.
For you know, they said, the black flies thrive
in darkness, in the shade of tombs, alive.

Never go into the cemetery at night, they said.
On this night of nights the full moon turns
the color of blood and rises with a glow,
like red ice from the gash on the hill.
Then it is the gravestone statues move in evil.
Prances then the iron horse while his headless master
hurls his lance with all his metal force
and will not miss you. He'll find out your heart.
For his venom for man and boy is a torch from Hell
and its scorching touch, like a scorpion's kiss, is death.

Oooh, in the dark of night on this night of nights
when the blood moon pales as it passes west,
new graves appear cut fresh and deep.
The hard earth splits with an opening hiss.
Beneath each fatal footstep that you take
dead old men arise, empty and eyeless,
with arms like steel clamps to pull you down
to their bony crypts, press you down
into their bony cages to sleep and sleep
and hug you tight till the earth shuts
over both them and you,
if you dare go into the graveyard at night.

Cold, cold is the Devil's moan, they said.
A stone would be warm if it's been in the sun.
If you enter the gates where they keep the dead,
and touch a stone and find it cold—
run, run, run, run, run.

V

It is important to keep the good memories.

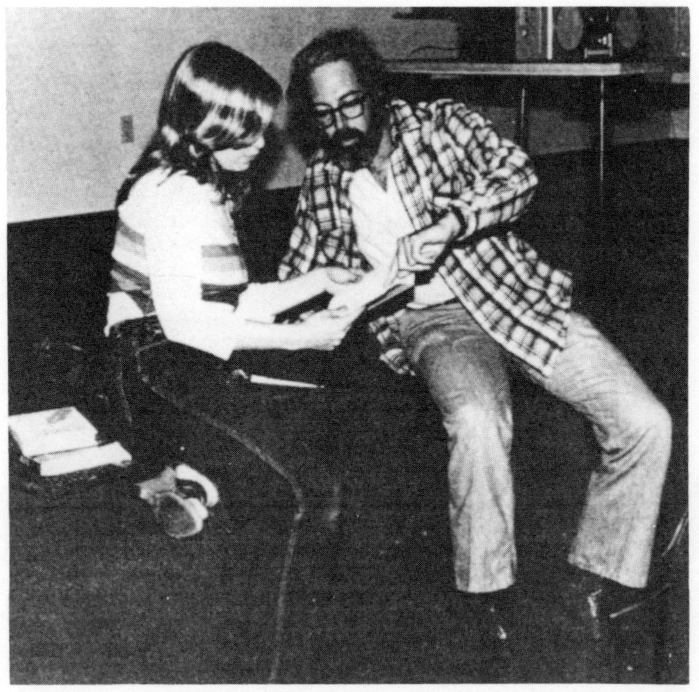

from: First Edition: 40 Poems

THREE COLORS

Butterflies in winter,
their delicate white wings
flutter to the ground.

In the evening snow
among sticks of the dark trees
a crow settles barely.

Green petals floating on still water.
Into the long night her eyes remain.

AFTER A HOT SHOWER

Facing an image in the mirror I live by it.
My face, our eyes, the levels of your tongue
suggest the subtle innuendo of a truth.
Distortion is somehow made reasonable.
Turning on my words I face the glass;
the fog hangs on it like a loose membrane,
cellular, peelable, tasting of lather and honey.
Run your fingers over it, I say emerging.
And my fingers pass over and against it.
The mist parts like a river and runs wetly down
streaming into lines as sharp as morning.
A smile appears (whose) and turns outward.
From under the stroke of your trembling finger streaks
    an eye.
It looks back on me. It is your eye,
it is mine, though there is but one eye
and it is strangely black
and very narrow.

BIRTHDAY 12:00 AM

Take your time,
keep dark, develop
slowly; maturation is
gradual. One has to build up courage
to leave the great immaculate heat.

Oh there
I'll tell you how it is: it's lovely,
other than the certain pressures from the outside,
poking, pushing, tapping, humping.
One gets used to it, yet
it's the actual growing that's of interest.
First thing you know you've got this tail.
You lay there sopping wet after a couple of months
and you have this tail.
All this in darkness.
                    Then, without warning,
bumps. A little arm here,
a possible leg there, boundless potential.
They shift around a bit, fuss and bother
in their rearrangement, and settle down.
Finally the head starts to swell
and the tail seems to suck itself
back up and in until
the very next thing you feel
is the receding of the hole.
Then it's done: psyche, footpads, shadow
and the substantial flesh of the shadow.

Consider the trauma, the confrontation, if you will.
A case in point: picture me sleeping
sound as any frog
curled in the enveloping folds of my natural hammock.

Suddenly I notice the great familiar pond of my youth
receding around me.
                         Half a dozen muffled screams
and a tap-tap. Like claws of some aluminum tiger
the forceps come wriggling in
clicking their silvery cold hooknails.
The pincers nip me on the ear and tangle
in my hair, they dart around
the startled wrinkles of my face.
                              Click-tap
click-tap
          They touch me and grab hold
around my head; I struggle, twisting
free. My leg is
caught,
bent, hot
head pushing. I grab into the peeling
membrane without teeth,
the stuff covers me
softening my fingers slicking them
the thin rubber fingers digging into my
groin   around my
neck   over my
face
mouth
filling and filling with curdling mucus
mouth nose eyes all one
and the trembling quick fingers ripping
me out into
the flickering lights
the insufferable freeze of the air
dankladen an noxious with sluffing
of tissue, life
                   the plantagenous fingers
crowd my tongue out
of my throat

       (breath) (breath)
and hoist
me backwards, gagging upwards, head reeling
down,
     over like...
           Hey!
           Did you ever have a little green frog
           held tight by its belly
           while you stuck it up its back
           with an iron needle?
           The legs sprang out and stiffened.
           Yes.
           But do you remember
           the scream?

           It went something like this:

YESTERDAY I FED THE FISH IN CITY PARK

From a half of leaning stump
I watched the minnows follow
a few crumbs in a trail. They'd jump
under any shadow
and if that shadow'd move
they'd move with it. Then my head
cast an image on their cover
and where it stayed they fed.
As if to eat my brain
fish mouths nibbled at the gray
between their air and mine.
And I sat. They ate all day.

THE CHINESE KITE

O prowler of the air, I see you
pulling your skirts in to slow
up a movement in air.
A papery drum comes rattling down,
hear it,
        frenzy, a green-eyed net,
falls on my ears: abide.

Tall is the dragon,
its stares higher than mountains.
Under the teetering strings I gallop.
Run, puppet,
your speed carries me.

Where there is fog heaven is
near enough to lick at.
A long path teases the cliff,
the place of our going.

I have climbed down from the encircling bridge
and have angled my walk like a sail in the wind.
The evening touches and moves on like a cloud—
Look! slack in the string.
I know the call—
        Catch hold, for I grow
heavy.

LAST DANCE AT WESTBROOK

It is cool and the crazy radio is sounding beautiful.
Every moment here shines, every moment glows,
glistens. I will not let go.

And Mary is a butterfly. I want her
to dance with me, fly around me,
dazzle the dying clock past sunrise.
"Would you dance, Mary? Will you dance?" I say,
and she rises on her bare toes like a colored moth,
rises from her cushioned chair
and moves out—how she turns and flutters
through the dim light. She is love
flying her pursuers, gently
tamping the tortures of her life down into the
    foundation.

I cannot keep my eyes on her
hands as they sway their slow frenzy.
"Where do your feet touch the ground? Show me."
I want the legs and arms of my body to be
what she is: to fly, be freedom, become symbolic.
My shod feet shuffle heavily on the linoleum.
My fist-like hand jerk, semi-clenched, cloddish.

The music goes on and it must go on.
I will learn this dance, to be nimble and easy,
but I cannot keep my eyes on her.
She is behind me, in front of me, beside me
in her ballet of being
while I watch shadows, punchy, loving
this rare moment of elusive grace.
"Mary Butterly," I say.
She smiles twisting away to the music.

You watch us from the couches and lounges caught
in the glow. I love you all
but at this moment, here, Mary is a silver moth
and it dances within me,
weaves magic circles, changes me, this moment,
this moment which is silver, because
it is all we have.

WHO WAS THAT GIRL

(for Susan S.)

I remember her
eyes, the dark look of them against the pillow,
the long hair, fine hair, untousled, smooth,
pale as her lips that spoke words I do not recall.

I do not remember her
words: they never came from her lips but came out
hard against the wall, against sheets of white paper,
struggling out, twisting out soft as a quiet shout.

I remember her
going away as she moved out of the light towards the
    empty street
and down towards the dark row of trees,
over the gravel path and off onto the grass with silent
    feet.

I do not remember her
feet making a sound, or ever coming back over the
    grass,
the strange words that stopped coming, or the wise
smile I saw just once as the light left her eyes.

movement

The turtle
is slow
as he crawls
to the
pond.

By the
time he
gets
there
the pond is
gone.

NABAGON

*It comes by thunder, rumbling and rolling
out of the north*

At Marblehead they know.
On the third night they know
it is the uneasy spirit of Nabagon
wailing at every rock and tree on the shoreline.
Where he was ripped by the razor talons,
stabbed through his bronze ribs by the long pale knives,
here the great black cougar spat and fought him
bleeding on the sand, and bled away,
one with the other battling back to heaven.

Building off Lake Erie the low breeze swirls quiet before
    the trees
then lifts from the water and rages.
Nabagon's sweet lover lies committed to the air.
The sweet woman of his death has bones of dust, is dust,
rock lips, stone heart, a mind of dark sediment.
She is dead. In the wild wind
the lost prince thunders emptily.
There is nothing left but the ragged cliff
where centuries have chopped a facial with a hollow
    mouth.

Green oaks froth like waves;
their broad summer leaves whip gray side up and scrape
as the wind hardens and hurtles upward from the white
    water
catching on rocks which conch-like deepen the echoes.

Sea birds cannot soar. Bees blow off course.
The tall stiff canvas on the lake boats buffet and shred
as men stand on the shore watching, huddled.
They breathe the violence in the air, know his voice,
do not turn their backs on it.

SUICIDE

Many times as a boy I leaped from Suicide
at Centennial Quarry. We tucked
our elbows rib tight to keep from overreaching.
Feet first or over forwards we feared
a bellysmack, or worse, the Crusher
when the dive was faulty.

You had to push off hard to get far out,
far enough over the rocks, but not too far,
and we all knew well the arc of the perfect
body was equal to the grab of the toes
plus the spring in the knees
less slippage on the little platform's narrow slats.
And if on a fast approach the ledge was slick
and the leap came off without gusto or guts,
if the arc went bad as the water hit...
Jesus, you never came up
and that was that.

VI

Some notes for a few poems.

A NOTE ABOUT THE NOTES

I like a reading where the poet talks about his poems as he says them. What he offers can be fascinating and personal and often makes an isolated poem comfortable. The poem can flow more out of the artist's own life.

No book can take the place of a live performance, of course. But this one can share some of the thoughts on some of the poems that are usually a part of my stand-up readings. I have tried not to interpret poems here. Instead I have written down a few of the private thoughts and experiences behind them.

"Blue Lovers": In the summer of 1982, I took the Blue Peanut (my eighteen foot motor home) west to the Olympic Peninsula with a lady named Krys. She believed in reincarnation and spoke of her past lives as if she were familiar with them. She also brought me into her cycle. We had been lovers many times and in different ages, she said. I was once her king.

I was interested not so much because of her belief but because others had told me the same thing, that centuries ago, perhaps before recorded history, I had been a king. Recently a friend asked me in what time in history I felt comfortable. I thought about it for awhile and said that I could see myself in sandals, wearing a long robe or tunic. And a staff, a tall walking stick had a good feel. Familiar. Yes, I could see myself perhaps in the days of Solomon, the Wise.

I had known a certain beautiful girl, Catholic-turned-Buddhist, in the Santa Monica Valley of California who went through regressive therapy to uncover the reason for her androphobia, her fear of men. Her therapist took her back through her past lives until she discovered that she had been an African male who had failed his tribal rite of initiation and was afraid to return to his village. The men found him hiding in the forest and brought him back to do the work of women, a shame until his death. When she discovered the reason for her fear, she overcame it.

Knowing this California girl's story, I listened to Krys with an open mind, but I still resisted the notion of reincarnation. The past was the past. The present, I thought, was what's meaningful. To me, a person's touch and warmth was far more real and believable than intuitive dreams, and a lot more comforting.

"Lovers": I see this poem as a celebration of the collective self, a Whitmanesque embrace of mankind and of nature. What it boils down to is this: there is a beauty beneath the skin which can bless each of us. We need to be receptive to the warmth of the soul and the spiritual essence of love that radiates from everyone.

"Poetry": In the spring of 1980, I was finishing the selection of manuscripts for the Cambric Press's *Poetry Project 2*. There was a cash prize for the best short poem and the final decision had to be made the following day. I took the poems home so I could divide them into two stacks, one for my volunteer reader and one for me.

My reader had been an A student in my poetry course. She was bright and had the rare ability to cut through obscurity and to feel and express the soul of a poem. But she was not only artistically sensitive, she was also sexy and she knew that I thought she was sexy. Whenever she came into my office, she wore paper-thin t-shirts and tourniquet-tight jeans. Around her twenty inch waist she would usually hook a thin macrame belt, unlatched and hanging. The end of it danced against the inside of her thighs as she walked. She told me that she had a lover just a few years younger than me and she detailed her weekends, what they did on the midnight beaches. You know. The focus was always on the tactile things that happened to her body. She knew what she was doing. Arousal without pity.

So while I worked that night on the poetry manuscripts, I decided to write a poem under a pseudonym and slip it in her stack as a late submission. She had heated/singed/burnt/fried my ears for a year and this was my chance to get even. I knew from the start that the basic metaphor would be about making love. The other level of the poem would use the vocabulary of poetry. Both these themes were high on my reader's list. I worked through the night.

The next morning at ten o'clock she walked in. Several hours later we had gone through the submissions. "Poetry" had made the semi-finals in her stack as I thought it might. An hour later she was still struggling over two poems, mine and one by a southern writer. I couldn't keep a straight face and told her that I was the author of "Poetry" and had written it with her in mind. She immediately chose the other poet.

"Bless Relaxes": In my first book I had a poem called "Oedipus Is A Bastard." It was a poem about guilt and the interruption of love and affection. "Bless Relaxes" is a reversal of that poem's tone and message. It came out of a conscious desire to alter the original through the new eyes of what I had become after my spirit search across the country in 1981 and 1982. The old poem is printed here for comparison, not out of fondness.

OEDIPUS IS A BASTARD

Swimming naked at the bottom of a wide blue pool
my students and I swim like dolphins.
Hours pass and not a ripple touches the mirror
top of water. Then there they are:
cold eyes peer out from behind a row of bricks.
They have the look of pebbles,
do not ask questions,
state merely facts.

I climb out of the pool into the eyes.
The students disappear, lovely.
The pool disappears.
The bricks are cold and hard.

I disappear.

"Walk": Only when one is ready to hear will he hear. And so
it was with me.

It was in August of 1981 that I met a song writer at
the Virginia Center for the Creative Arts. Susan was
direct and spoke with the authority of infinite
knowledge and common sense reinforced by passionate
conviction. One evening after we had visited the Edgar
Casey Institute in Virginia Beach, she asked me to
describe my marriage. What I conjured up for her was a
fifteen year ordeal, a perpetual downward deadening
relationship.

I had talked about my marital problems with other
friends and they always said the same thing, "Get out of
it." But I never did anything. Yet when this stranger,
Susan, simply said, "There's only one thing to do.
Walk!" as if it were the only possible move in the world,
I said "Yes." Yes, I knew she was right as I had known
the others were right. What was different was that when
I said yes, it was done. In an instant, I had completed
the divorce myself, I had freed myself. The time had
come. That evening I made the simple life-changing
decision that had been an agony to me for years.

When I came back to Ohio to tell my wife, she agreed
without a flinch or twitch and a hundred elephants flew
from my shoulders and bubbled about the sun. A fan-
tasy had come true. Yes.

"Sketch 2": The Pyramids of the Sun and the Moon are like
mighty bookends. These two huge structures create the
walkway called the Valley of the Dead at Teotihuacan
near Mexico City. The day I was there, March 20, 1978,

the sun was supposed to pass directly over them. It was hot and the sky was liquid fire. If you had fair skin and weren't covered, you burned.

One of the women with our little group was young and angry. Life was not an adventure for her; it was a bitch. She looked but was blind; she touched but never felt. As we walked together down the Valley of the Dead, I thought I saw the begging children as extensions of her mind.

"Flames": In 1977, I went to the Interlochen National Music Camp near Traverse City, Michigan, with my two daughters. One afternoon while they were building sand castles on the beach, the girl of my summer dreams materialized. Dark hair, brown eyes, soft low voice that could calm a sea, the oldest daughter of one of the music instructors. She was working that summer in the snack bar from five until closing. She made friends with my girls and was comfortable with me. Later we went over and bought milkshakes from her.

That night after the girls were asleep I had a terrible need to get out of the cabin. Despite my wish to do otherwise, I found myself almost driven back to the snack bar. I tried to turn back, but I couldn't. This is stupid, I said to myself, and yet there I was, circling closer and closer to the brightly lit glass building in the center of the campus's web of concrete walkways. I felt biologically helpless.

I sat on a bench outside the stand and watched the girl make cones, joke with co-workers, finally close up and flick off the flourescent lights. My heart was pounding as she came out of the side exit. I wanted to hug her, squeeze her, walk her back to her cabin, touch her, be touched, listen to her voice. But I sat there, both pulled and riveted, heart throbbing with desire and humiliation. I watched her walk away down one of the dim concrete paths into the darkness of the trees. I sat alone in the dark and cursed myself for being such a miserable joke. It was a bad time.

"The Bed": I returned to Huron in March 1982. My almost-ex-wife had found me a furnished garret on the third floor of a fine old house on Center Street. My three rooms were small and brightly painted. The bedroom, for example, had walls and ceiling that were a continuous lime green. It took a few days to get used to it, especially after having only a tiny sleeping space in the Blue Peanut (See note to "Blue Lovers") and I came to like the room. In the spring mornings the east window dripped with dew and the sun reflected into the room through white gauze curtains bathing everything in the same intense green glow I had seen in the rain forests of southeast Alaska.

The bed in the green room was a dilapidated double. The mattress was old and sunken in the middle. Only two slats held up the collapsed box spring. But strangely enough, it was comfortable, like a nest. I had never liked soft beds but this one was different.

Out of curiousity one day, I asked Harriet, my landlady, who had stayed in the room before me. That's when she told me about the young man who had gone on a starvation diet until he got so malnourished that he had to be taken away. He didn't die but the possibility of it struck me one night as I lay in the faded contours of his evaporated body.

Late in November, Harriet took the bed out and put in a newer one. I felt a loss. It had been as comfortable as an old pair of sneakers.

This draft is dated December 5, 1982. The first draft was started while the old bed was still a part of the green forest light.

"I Was Thinking of Apples": This poem has nothing to do with losing a lover, but that's what caused it. I was determined to avoid self-pity and grief and to focus on happy things the night the relationship bottomed. I was never going to get back into that Interlochen frame of mind. (See "Flames" note above.) And so for no particular reason I chose to write about one of my favorite objects, apples. Better yet, apple pie. The syllables were so juicy and I was so happy over the poem's sound that I called my ex-lover and read it to her. "That's nice," she said. "Goodbye." That night I went to sleep with a smile. The poem sang me to sleep.

"Time Is All I Need": I call this a progressive chant. I had written "Solo I Will Stand in the Winds That Choose to Take Me" a year before and this poem takes sound experimentation in a different direction. I use repetition of key words, then let the words flow into new but related ideas and phrases which, in turn, I pick up with their own repetitions.

I try to keep my poems concrete in imagery, but sometimes the sound of a word becomes the dominant image. I think that is what happens in this poem.

"Solo I Will Stand in the Winds That Choose to Take Me": Years ago I saw a documentary film in which Louis Zukovsky read a poem he had created from a line of Shakespeare. I don't recall the poem but I do remember its refrain, "Come, shadow, come..." It was an experiment in repetitive sound that excited me.

In October of 1980, I was talking about quatrains in a poetry class and thought I would see what I could do to expand Zukovsky's idea. I wanted repeatable title words that would remain interesting, words that were short and monosyllabic, words easy to transpose and manipulate. I took several days to make the selection. When the title was set, I began to chant it, mixing its words. Suddenly the lines began to flow. By my own rules, the twelve words of the title could be repeated or dropped out of any line, but no new word could be added. Even the verb form had to remain unchanged.

The first time I said this poem to a group, I felt electricity. The poem came out as a chant. I had just returned to teaching after nine weeks on my back from spinal surgery. The evening I read this poem I was too weak to stand, but in spite of my almost inaudible and painful seated delivery, the sounds and words captured my listeners. "A religious experience," one of the women there told me afterwards. Maybe it was.

In September of 1981, I was in Manitowoc, Wisconsin, to give a reading at Silver Lake College. I asked my host and friend, Father Jim Massart, if I could borrow a kettle drum from the college's music department. When I arrived for the reading, it was waiting for me. I used it in "Solo"'s presentation and, when I interrupted the verbal chant at certain stanza breaks with the deep drum's own ritualistic sound, the poem became for me a Mighty Poem.

"Hush, the Girls Are Sleeping": Good and evil. God and Satan. Life and death. Inner peace and the chaos of the outer world. Natural sounds and the inharmonious cacophony of clashing gears. Stasis and movement. A mountain of opposites and polarities shaded this poem. They emerged naturally as the poem began to develop on the page and in my mind, yet the way they remained was unnatural. At least for me.

I need to sketch two scenes and tell you how the ideas in this poem came to be:

Scenario One. It is October 1977. I have just come home from teaching a night class. It is about 9:30 p.m. My wife has gone to work and my daughters have been in bed for an hour. I am not yet exhausted but am getting close to it. It is quiet in the house. I am sitting in the comfortable padded

90

father-chair near the foot of the stairs in the living room. I pull my legs up under me and sit cross-legged, breathing deeply to blow out the tensions of the day.

I am thinking this night about my poetry and about the trend I have been following. My first book has been out almost two years and I recall the burden of negative feelings that make up so much of it. I think also of the poems I have completed and have been working on since that publication. Pretty somber stuff. Joyless and brown. I am tired of doing dark passages and I say to myself, "I want to do more poems like "Last Dance at Westbrook.' There's a glimpse of joy in that one." But my other poems do not rise to the joy around me.

I ask myself, "Can I turn it around? Can I write a poem of Joy?" And so I give myself an assignment: to write about something beautiful and not to get out of the chair until a first draft is done.

I am sitting in the father-chair thinking these thoughts now under a self-imposed mandate. I am waiting for an idea. Suddenly I am aware of heavy breathing at the top of the stairs. My daughters are up there deep in sleep. Their inhaling-exhaling becomes louder as I focus in on them and although they are breathing out of rhythm, the sounds they blow down to me become music.

Scenario Two: A second influence adds to the foundation of "Hush." A year earlier I made a trip to Las Vegas, Nevada. There is a convention at Caesar's Palace and I am also booked to read poetry at the University of Nevada campus. After the reading two graduate students offer to drive me into the desert that makes Nevada a place of beauty. Along the way, they tell me stories of assassinations and how, once in awhile, prospectors or dune-buggy freaks find a bullet ridden body stripped of identification and covered with rocks, or a carcass which is crushed and split from being dumped out of a midnight Cessna. Gruesome stories. Part of the area's criminal folklore.

After a twenty mile drive, we turn off Charleston onto a gravel road which leads back into Red Rock Canyon. Huge boulders surround the turn-around where we stop and my hosts suggest that we do a little rock climbing. They want to show me the real desert and its silence. From the top of a mountainous pile of boulders, I see vast miles of rocks, scrub brush and sand. Way off in the distance is the highway and at the end of it, going away, an eighteen-wheeler trailing a long shadow cast by the evening sun. Long after the truck has disappeared I can hear the whine of its wheels as they spin over the concrete into the purpling mountains. And then...

As the sound of the truck vanishes, there comes that devastating silence they have talked about. I become aware of a low thunder bouncing around, some violent echo of civilization trapped in my head. I cannot get rid of it and the more I am aware of it the louder it becomes. Finally I clap my hands over my ears and grit my teeth. What I have is more than a headache; it is the fear of of permanent contamination. I have touched a new level of awareness and I am shocked by the realization that my ears carry their own noise.

End of scenarios.

Still in my chair, I flashed back on the red red rocks, the miles of desert and cold mountains, the unutterable silence which forced the poison of noise out of my ears. And the tales of murder. All that I had experienced in the desert boiled up in me as I sat there a year later. But remember, I was going to write a poem about something beautiful. What was beautiful at that moment was the breathing and the lives of my girls sleeping above me.

The first lines started out all right. They had the tone I wanted. The girls were the subject. Their breathing was the dominant image that worked itself easily into the mystery of life I was feeling at the moment. But suddently the beauty vanished as I became aware instead of trucks passing on U.S. 2 a couple blocks away. It was when I first tuned out the breathing coming down to me and into the loud engines outside that I realized the structure of the poem. I decided to let the poem flow; I would try to block nothing. Let it come.

A stanza of truck noise got onto the paper. (Not the one which is in the poem now, but one similar to it). And then I stopped. "Wait," I said to myself. "Get back to the beauty. Allow the flow but don't let it take over, don't let it control." The last thing I wanted was a poem with more negative imagery. And so, despite the fact that I was going to just be passive, I forced myself back to the girls. And so another stanza worked its way onto the paper. Then again my mind unfixed and I found myself back in the desert with the rocks, the silence, the day's heat and the night's cold. The desert pit vipers are the classic symbol of evil, for the greed and corruption I had seen and heard about. The snake became a dominant image in this poem about angels. The second polarity emerged.

In the last two stanzas, lost, I find myself saved by the voices, the breaths. My salvation. This was what I was searching for when I began the poem. It wasn't the means I had envisioned but the end was close. There was something of beauty here, and the beauty, to my surprise, came from the contrast.

When I finished the first draft, it was 4:30 in the morning.

For a long time afterwards, years in fact, I toyed with the idea of editing the poem to take out the negative. But the results were unsatisfactory. It wasn't the same. It was flat. The more I thought about it, the more I realized that the strength of the poem, for me anyway, lay in the struggle going on on the page. The tension between good and evil grew as the poem was being created; the evil kept wedging into my original intent and I decided, once and for all time, to let the poem stand as it was composed.

This is an important poem for me. It records the memory of a love and a rekindling of that love. Two small children and a father alone together, and I the guardian of their innocence. Despite other outside influences, it was a good moment in our lives.

"Sitting for Margaret": I met Margaret Christy in 1975. Her daughter was taking creative writing from me and one class met at her home. All the art in the house had been done by Margaret. After class, she pulled out a large folio of charcoal portraits she had done the summer before in South America. All her subjects were old, most were in their hundreds. At that time, I was editor of the *Firelands Review* and I asked if we could feature her work in the bicentennial edition. Margaret thrust her collection into my arms and told me to choose whatever I wanted. In 1977, 1978 and 1979 I reprinted a few more.

She retired from teaching and had set up a year long sketching trip across Canada and down the West Coast, but before she left she wanted to do a portrait of me. On the appointed day, she came to my office with her sketch pad. I sat for several hours but when the preliminary drawing was done she didn't like it. Something, she said, was eluding her. At five o'clock we both had had enough and she went home to work on it.

A week later she was back. She wanted to start over.

So I sat for another two hours. Again she wasn't happy with the drawing. That night she phoned me. She had touched up and altered the new sketch but it had a strange look of sadness that she couldn't get out. A third sitting was impossible because of time but I could have the portrait, she said, or I could throw it away. She dropped it off the next day and left for the northwest.

I looked at my portrait. The hair was good, but the eyes, nose and mouth seemed to be someone else's. And I was sure I had been smiling, at least a little. But it wasn't in the picture. I didn't throw the drawing away. I filed it.

Margaret was somewhere in California when the 1980 *Firelands Review* came up for printing. While looking through my portfolio I came across her sketch. Just the day before a friend and I had been talking about the differences between the artist's intent and his work's outcome. Our dialog clicked with Margaret's portrait. This poem started to generate itself as I tried to capture the frustration she felt as she worked. The 1980 Review came out with Margaret's portrait of me; this poem was printed on the opposite page.

"Discharge from the Asylum": Despite the somber tone of this poem, its genesis was humorous and ironic. I was just returning from my sabbatical, eight months of travel, development and self-indulgence. At 6:30 in the morning on St. Patrick's Day I left Banner Elk, North Carolina. I drove through the Blue Ridge Mountains shrouded in dense fog. I arrived in Johnson City, Tennessee, an hour later. There, in front of a McDonald's Restaurant, I was side-swiped by an old Ford sedan. Twenty-six thousand miles without a scratch and now, on the last day out, my left side from rear to front, was a sheet of folded, twisted metal. The man who hit me was a local and there was no citation. Somehow Blue Peanut was driveable and I drove slowly and steadily up

Interstate 75 to Bowling Green where I planned to spend the night.

T.L., a friend of mine, had fixed me up with one of her co-workers. I really wasn't ready for a date; I was beat after the drive and trauma of the accident, but I wasn't going to let one bad day wipe away a whole good year and so we went out for a drink, Mona and I, to get to know each other. I found out that she worked with mentally retarded adults.

It was cold and rainy that night and after we left Milton's Bar, Mona asked me if I'd like to sleep in her cottage rather than in the back of my r.v. The heater hadn't been working and it was cold so I said yes, having no expectation of what was to come.

We drove to the town of Portage, down a small road, and turned into a parking lot flanked by neat brick buildings. She hushed me as we got out and said we'd wake the cottagers if we were too loud. We tiptoed down a dim linoleum hallway to her apartment. It was late and Mona pulled out a hideabed for me, gave me some blankets and a pillow, said goodnight, and disappeared into her bedroom. "Well," I said to myself, "this is the end of the trip." And I went to sleep.

I woke up to screaming out in the hall. Mona's bedroom door was open and she was gone. What I was hearing was a dozen M.R.'s in the bathroom, washing up for the day. Screaming, crying, laughing, yelling, cooing, taunting. And so my odyssey of growth ended in a madhouse. I was out of there in half an hour.

"O O Wonder Woman": My thanks to actress Lynda Carter, who played Wonder Woman on the television series in the '70's.

"Red Water Mite": There was a small pond off a hidden dirt road about twenty miles north of Fairbanks, Alaska. I discovered it late in June, around the time of the vernal

equinox. The first time I stopped there I went down to
the edge of the water and bent close to see if there was
any animal life. There were thousands of moving ob-
jects, euglena, paramecium and other microscopic mat-
ter but the one creature that caught my eye was a red
mite.

I watched the wee speck's rapid pulse-like out-
thrashing from ten in the morning until late in the after-
noon. It never stopped. I squatted till my knees got stiff,
then I knelt until they hurt. Finally I lay on my belly in
the dirt. Something about this animal, no bigger than
the head of a pin, fascinated me, and I knew this was a
precious moment in my life. I had no idea why, but I
knew it was.

For the seven hours I watched, the mite swam without
making an inch of headway. I left the spot for a minute
to relieve myself behind a bush, but when I came back
to the edge of the pond, it was gone.

I knew that some day when the time was right
something would come of this, a poem or an epic novel.
The poem came fourteen years later after more bad
starts than I care to count.

"Denali": After I graduated from college in 1960, I left the
"lower 48" to go to the University of Alaska near Fair-
banks. There were fewer than 600 students then and
many of them were from other universities. What
brought a lot of them was Denali. Denali was known un-
til 1980 as Mt. McKinley. Young climbers and
photographers from all over the world came to study
and to prepare to scale its notorious slopes.

I never did climb this great mountain, but I did climb
mountains further south. In August of 1961, I was hired
as a packer and assistant guide on one of Hal Waugh's
inland hunting expeditions. After we were dropped by
seaplane at our remote base camp at Post Lake on the
south fork of the Kuskokwim River, we set out after

Dahl sheep. On the third day, we spotted a string of rams on a far mountain slope and we took off downwind after them. We were in the Alaskan Range three more days on that chase and I'll never forget the sight of them, snow white against the shale outcroppings, moving like tiny ships under canvas across invisible mountain paths. It was their land, their kingdom. We shouldn't have been there. But we were and it is now one of the sweetest memories of my life.

"The City Brother and the Country Brother": In the mid-'70's, urban renewal desecrated Huron, Ohio. City council decided, despite opposition, to level all the old buildings, the wooden stores with slat floors that smelled of age. Every building with character on Main Street (except a bank, a telephone company circuit office, a beer carry-out, a mortuary and the Catholic Church) came crashing down under the raping impact of demolition balls. Tradition and the comfort of familiarity fell to the sterile council's clever Blitzkrieg motto: :"A New Huron for a New Time."

Not only were whole blocks razed and turned to brick-strewn rubble, but the council wanted to begin a multi-million project to construct a small boat marina on Main Street. Thus, a huge bite was gouged out of the shoreline in the middle of town and Main Street was cut in half. The town looked like a war zone. In effect, Huron was gone.

It was at this time that my brother Jon came to visit from Chicago. At suppertime he and I drove across the battlefield for a couple of pizzas. We passed the broken buildings and the ruined streets. He commented on the silence, the absence of pedestrians, the emptiness. On the way back, we came across a couple in their eighties wearing jogging suits. They were standing on a little bridge over a drainage pipe staring down at the shallow water. Jon was fascinated by them and stared at them as we went by. He didn't say anything, he just stared.

We had supper, talked awhile, and then he drove back to Chicago. The poem began to emerge about a week later.

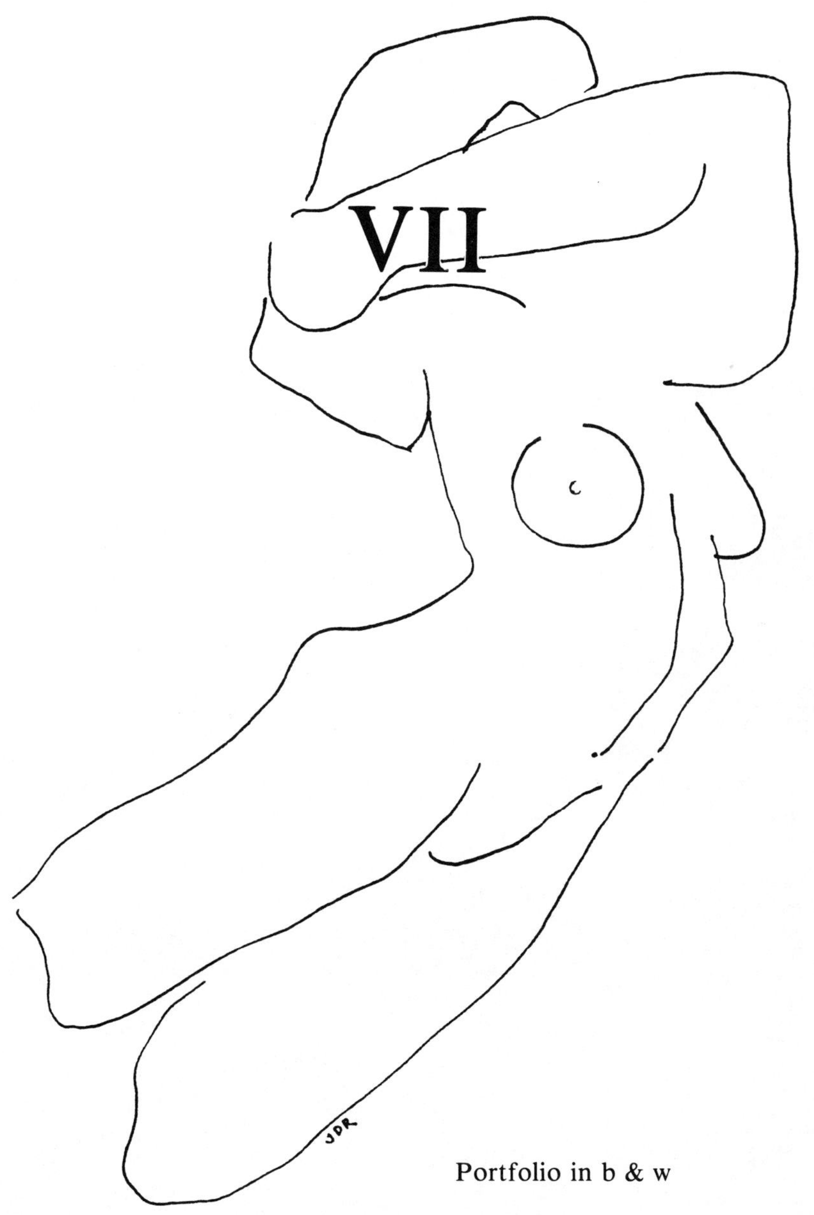

Portfolio in b & w

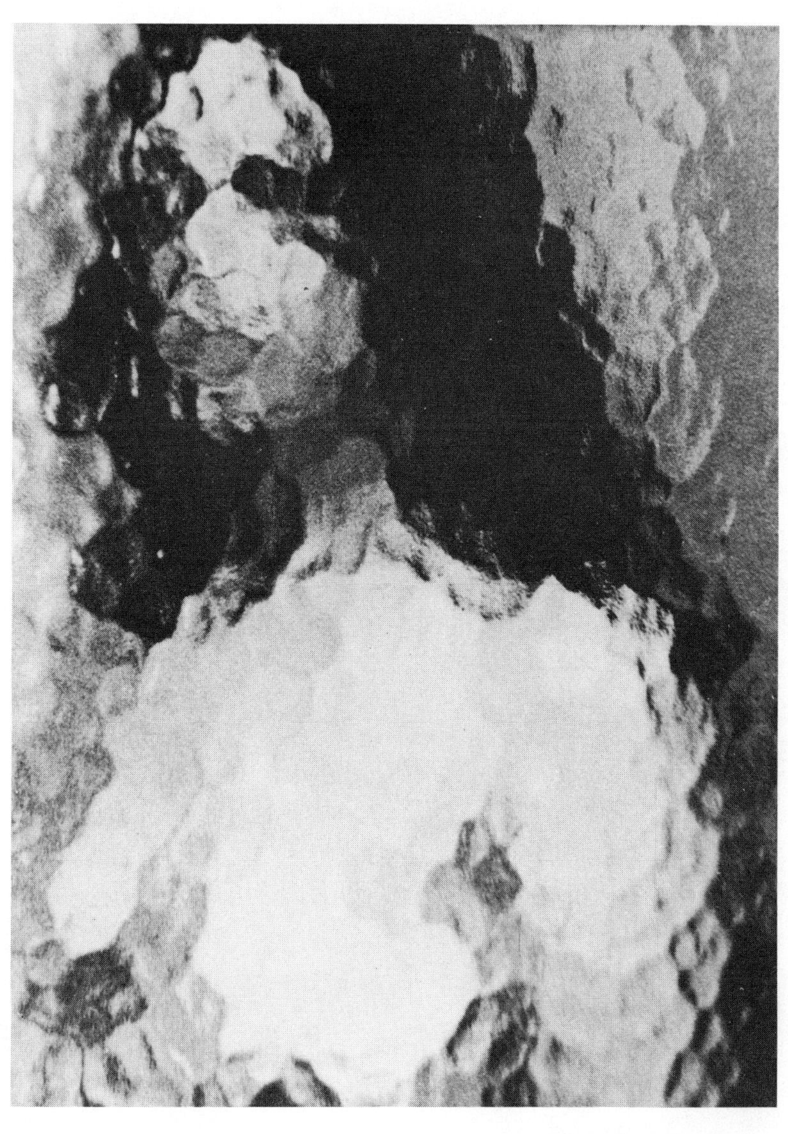

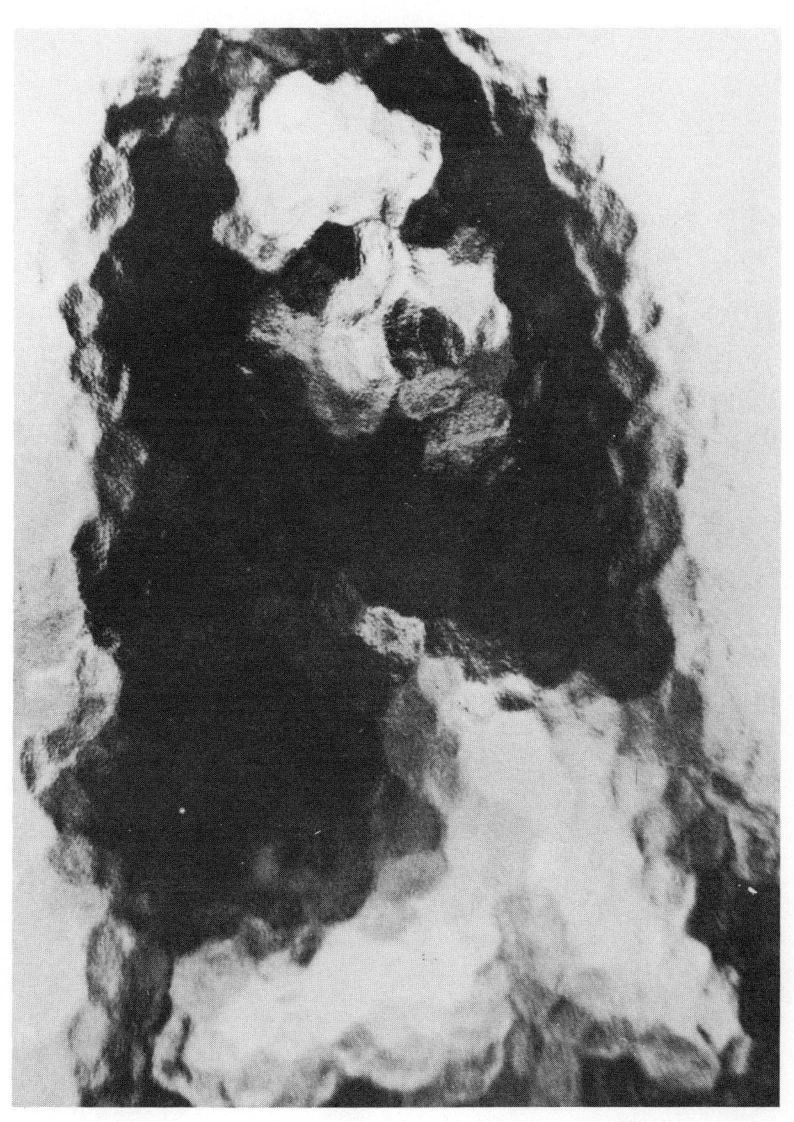

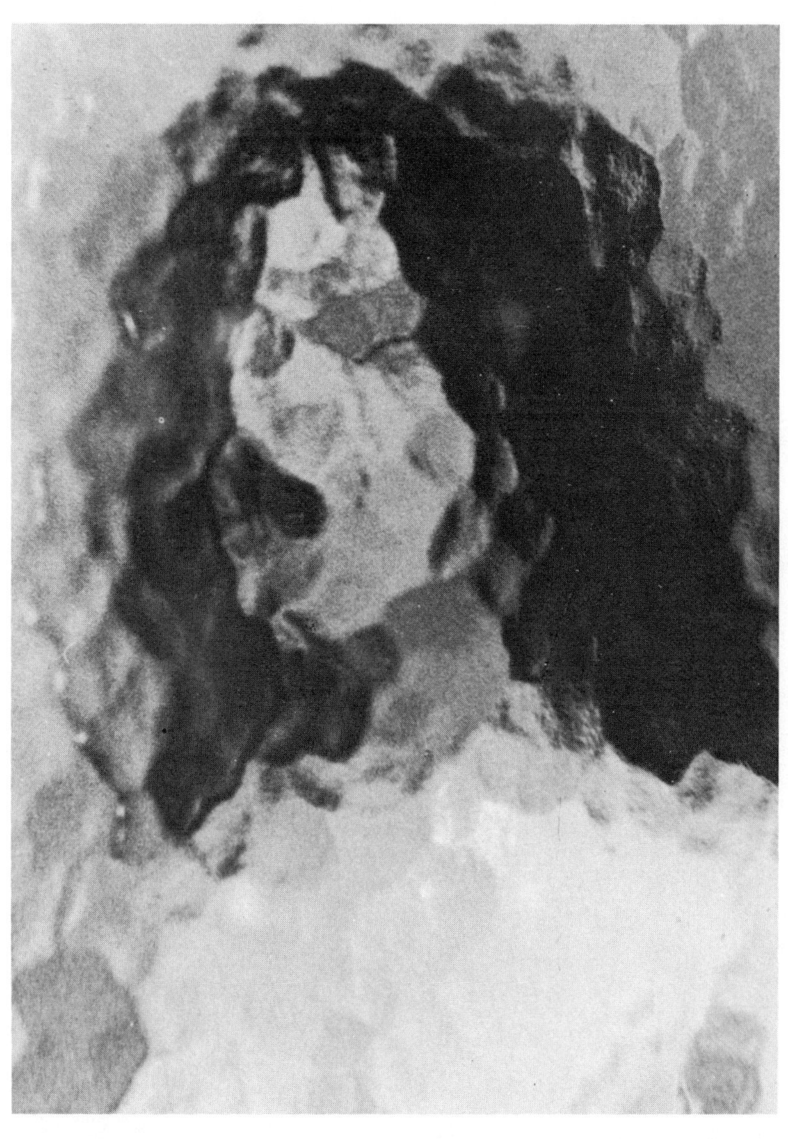

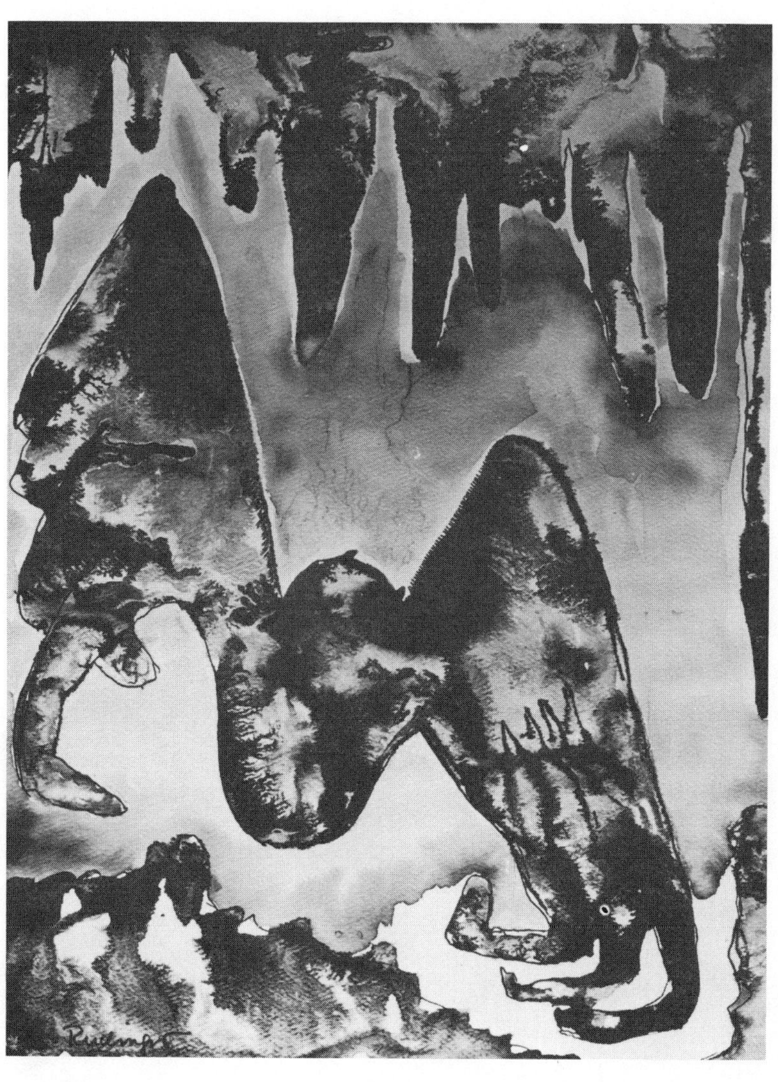

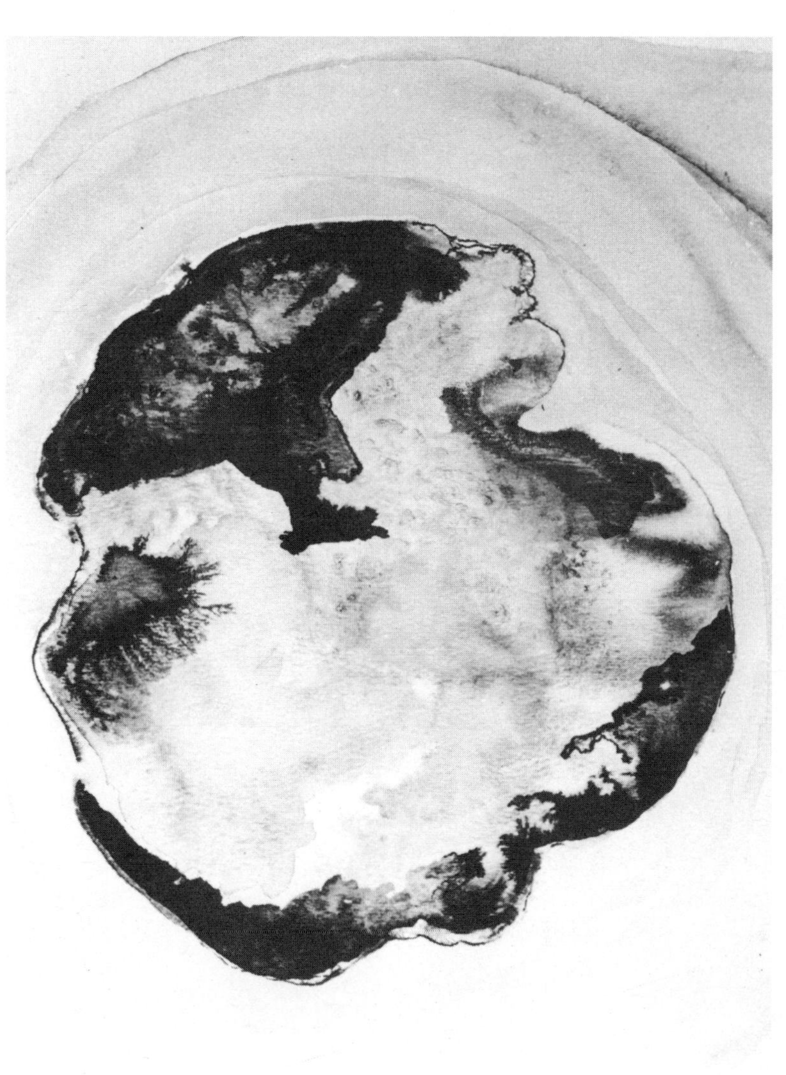

RUDINGER

Morning After   Ruanger '52

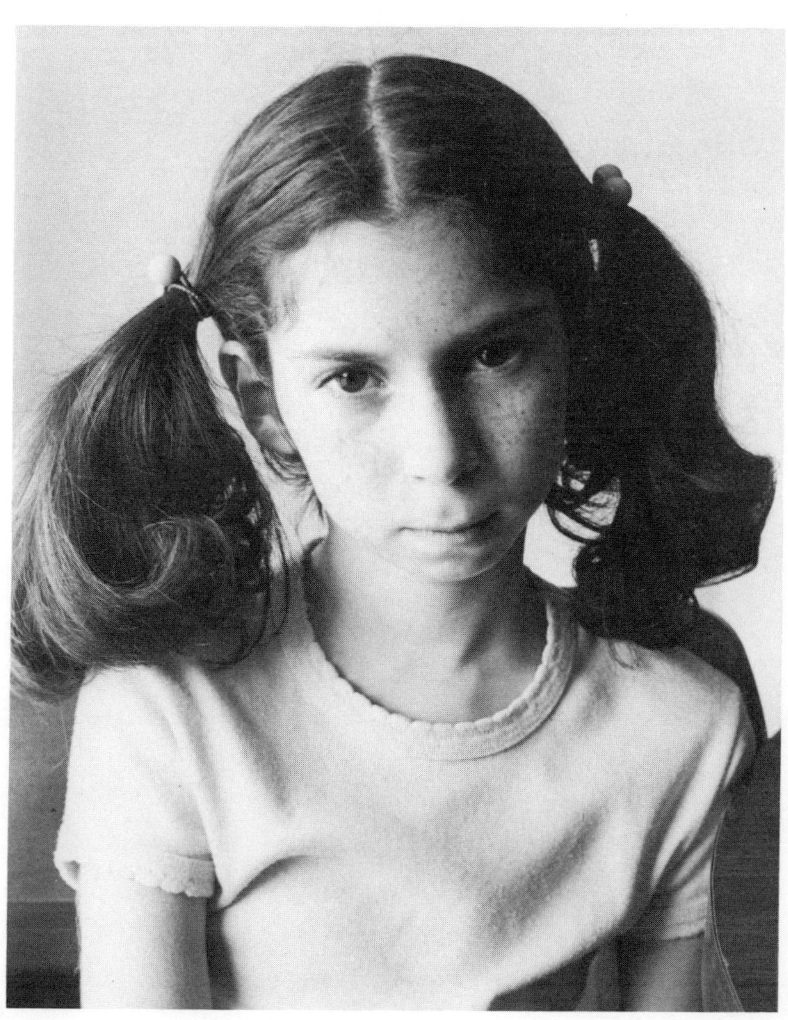